The UL... Magic Club

Magnetic Magic!

by Danny Orleans and John Railing

Professional Magicians

Scholastic Inc.

New York   Toronto   London   Auckland   Sydney   Mexico City   New Delhi   Hong Kong   Buenos Aires

ISBN 0-439-80338-1
Copyright © 2005 by Scholastic Inc.

Design: Mark Neely and Michaela Zanzani
Studio photography: James Levin
Hair and makeup: Kathy Morano
Other photo credits:
Page 27: (left and center) Courtesy of Hermetic Press;
(top right) The Nielsen Poster Collection.

12 11 10 9 8 7 6 5 4 3   5 6 7 8 9/0

Printed in China
First printing, December 2005

★ Table of Contents ★

★ = easy magic trick   ★ = more challenging trick   ★ = really challenging trick!

✶ A Magical ✶ Attraction!

Change a penny into a dime. Make a ball appear under a cup. Transform a black-and-white chip into a blue-and-green one. What do all these amazing tricks have in common? Magnets!

You may not be able to *see* the little tricksters, and that's a good thing—because then your audience won't see 'em either. That's why it'll be easy to fool your friends when you're doing the "forceful" tricks featured in *Magnetic Magic*!

Watch the Attraction in Action!

All the secret moves you need to know to pull off each trick are explained right here in this book. If you're wondering how each trick should look, or what you should say when you perform for an audience, just pop in your DVD, and you'll see the tricks demonstrated by the Ultimate Magic Club magicians shown on the left.

Watch the videos carefully and practice each secret move, and soon you'll be "attracting" lots of attention with your magnetic magic!

Alvaro

Leah

Cristian

Amy

Sofie

Mpho
(pronounced
EM–po)

The Ultimate Magic Club

Magnetic Magic!
©2005 Scholastic Inc.

What's in Your MaGic Kit?*

PENNY TRANSFORMER SET

The penny shell that comes with this set might *look* ordinary on one side, but just flip it over, and you'll see that it's only a hollow shell! It has steel in it, which means it'll stick to the red magnet. When you hide things underneath the penny shell, you can make magical transformations happen with a tap of the red magnet! Just turn to page 6 to find out how to turn a penny into a dime!

Penny shell

Magic cup (with magnetic bottom)

Normal ball

Copper Blob
Hide this under your penny shell to make it look like you've melted a penny!

Red magnet

MAGIC CUP and BALLS

One of the two balls in this set has a very sneaky secret—it has a metal core, which means it'll stick to the bottom of the magnetic cup. You can use this secret to pull off all sorts of fun tricks. Learn the first one by turning to page 18!

Trick ball (with metal core)

COLOR-CHANGING CHiPS

Thanks to hidden magnets, this pair of black-and-white chips will suddenly turn into colorful chips, right before your friends' eyes! All it takes is a pair of metal disks that hide the colors until you do some secret moves. Flip to page 14 to see how simple it is!

Metal disks

Reset magnet

MiNi-MAGNET

What's small, powerful, and part of your Magnetic Magic kit? Your mini-magnet, of course. Team it up with a bandage on your finger, and you can use it to turn pennies into dimes, make paper clips stick to a paper magnet, stop watches, and lots more. The mini-magnetic fun begins on page 10!

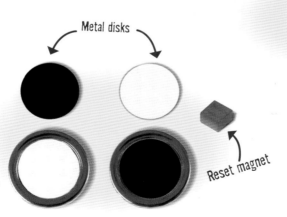

Change for a Penny

A penny won't buy you much these days—but if you could change pennies into dimes, *then* you'd be in business! Try this simple little trick with your Penny Transformer Set, and turn a penny into a dime in an instant!

you'll need...

* **Penny Transformer Set**
* **Dime**

Penny shell   Red magnet

get ready

Put the dime on a table and cover it with the penny shell. You're ready to roll!

make magic!

1 Slowly pass the red magnet over the penny shell. The magnet should be very close to the penny shell—less than half an inch above it.

2 When the magnet is right above the penny shell, the shell will jump up and cling to the bottom.

The penny shell sticks to the magnet.

3 Move the magnet away, and the dime will come into view. The transformation is complete!

EXTRA CREDIT

After you do this trick, some people may want to see the bottom of the red magnet. What should you do?

If you're sitting at a table, you can try this:

1. As soon as your friends see the dime, push it toward them and tell them to check out both sides to make sure the transformation really worked. While your friends are looking at the dime, they won't be looking at you!
2. Use this opportunity to quickly brush the shell off the magnet and into your lap. Just hold the magnet on the edge of the table and brush the shell off with your fingers or thumb. It'll land quietly in your lap.
3. Then put the magnet on the table so your friends can look at it. Nothing there!

The Brush-Off Move

tip Don't look at the magnet or your lap when you do the Brush-Off Move. Watch this trick on your DVD to see how quick and casual it should be!

Penny Melt

It takes lots of heat to melt a copper penny, right? Wrong! All it takes is a little magic. In this trick, your Penny Transformer Set unites with the copper blob to create a magical meltdown!

you'll need...

* Penny Transformer Set
* Copper blob

Copper blob

tip Run warm water over the copper blob before the trick so it'll feel freshly melted!

get ready

Put the copper blob on a table and cover it with the penny shell.

make magic!

This is easy! Just put the red magnet on top of the penny shell and then lift it off. The penny has melted!

More Penny Magic

What *else* can you do with your Penny Transformer Set? Lots! Try these ideas, and then invent some of your own penny magic!

A Penny Mystery

Hide a real penny somewhere (like inside a book, under a potted plant, or in the freezer), and then write that location on a tiny strip of paper. Fold the paper in half and place it under the penny shell.

Then use your red magnet to make the penny shell disappear. When your friends ask where the penny went, have them read the strip of paper and go find the penny!

Try hiding the penny under a chair or inside a book!

UNDER CHAIR

ON PAGE 97

 tip Make sure the real penny matches the color of the penny shell.

Penny-trate

Put a penny in your shoe, then put on the shoe and lace it up.

When you're ready to perform, place the penny shell on top of your shoe. Then use the red magnet to make the penny shell disappear. Where'd the penny go? Take off your shoe and show everyone!

Turn a Penny into a Fortune!

Make a fortune appear under your penny shell! To do this, trace the outline of the penny shell onto a piece of paper, and then cut out a circle inside the line (so the paper will fit underneath the shell). Use a sharpened pencil to write a tiny fortune, and then sneak it under the penny shell.

When you're ready to perform, lay the red magnet on the penny shell and tap three times. Lift the magnet, and there's the fortune!

Heads or Tails?

Can you turn a tails-up penny into a heads-up penny just by tapping it with your fingers? You *can* if you use your penny shell and a tiny magnet hidden under a bandage! Watch the puzzled looks on your friends' faces when you stack up a bunch of pennies and "flip over" the top one with a quick tap!

you'll need...

* Mini-magnet
* Bandage
* Penny shell
* Nine pennies

Penny shell

Mini-magnet

get ready

1 Place the mini-magnet on one of the sticky sides of the bandage.

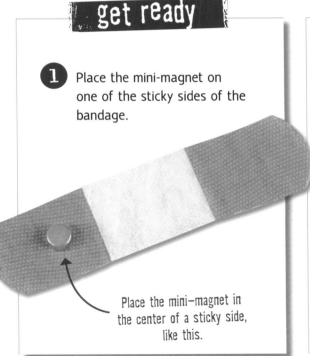

Place the mini-magnet in the center of a sticky side, like this.

2 Put the middle section of your third finger on the mini-magnet and wrap the bandage around your finger.

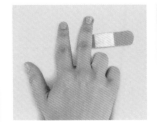

make magic!

1 Place your pennies in a group on a table. Make sure to keep track of which one is the penny shell!

Penny shell

2 Stack up all the pennies except for the penny shell. The ninth penny should be heads up.

Make sure this penny is heads up.

Penny shell

3 Then put the penny shell on top of the stack, making sure that no one sees the fake side!

4 Tell your friends to look at the top penny and notice which side is up. Then do the next few steps very quickly!

5 Hold your hand flat (fingers together) and lightly tap the bandaged finger on the penny shell.

The penny shell will stick to the hidden magnet!

6 Pull your hand (and the penny shell) away.

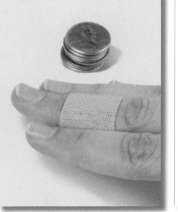

7 Then rest your hand on the edge of the table. While your friends are looking at the penny on top of the stack, brush off the penny shell with your thumb and let it drop quietly into your lap!

More Magic with Your Mini-Magnet

When you hide your mini-magnet under a bandage on your finger, there's lots of magnetic magic you can do. Try shrinking a stack of pennies by making one disappear. Or try making a compass needle whirl round and round. You can even stop time! Here are just a few *attractive* ideas!

Shrink a Stack

Stack up eight pennies, counting them as you go. Make sure that the penny shell is on top. Also make sure that the real penny under it is the same color as the penny shell and is also tail side up.

When you tap the stack with your bandaged finger (secretly stealing the penny shell), your audience won't notice a difference—until they count the pennies for themselves and realize that one's disappeared! (While they're busy counting, slip the penny shell into your pocket.)

Change Your Change

Place a bunch of coins on a table—including at least three dimes and three pennies. Now place the penny shell on top of one of the dimes. Ask a friend to add up all the money without touching the coins. Then wave your hand over the coins and say, "Change my change!" When your friend counts the money again, there'll be nine cents more!

Stop Watch

If you have a watch with a moving second hand, you can stop time! Just hold the watch in your fingers and slowly let your mini-magnet get close to the back of the watch.

As you wave your other hand over the watch's face, suddenly the second hand will stop. Then wave your hand again as you move your bandaged finger—just a little bit—away from the watch. The second hand will be free to tick again! (Don't worry—this won't hurt the watch!)

Penny to Dime— Another Way!

You can use your mini-magnet to change a penny to a dime *without* the red magnet. Just cover a dime with your penny shell, as shown on page 6. Then wave your bandaged finger over the penny shell, and you've turned a penny into a dime with your bare hands!

To get rid of the evidence, use the Brush-Off Move shown on page 7. Make sure to ask your friends to check out the dime so you'll have a moment to do the move when they're not watching!

Which Way is Which?

Why does a compass needle point north? It's because the needle is magnetic, and it's responding to the Earth's magnetic field. This means you can *really* "confuse" a compass by bringing a magnet close to it! Here's how you can make it look like magic:

1. Put the bandage with the mini-magnet on your ring finger near the tip.

2. Hold the compass between your thumb and index finger. Spread your fingers out so the magnet is as far away from the compass as possible. Patiently wait for the needle to be very still.

3. Then slowly move your bandaged finger toward the compass. You won't have to move far to make the needle jump and spin. At the same time, wave your other hand over the compass, saying that your strong magic powers will confuse the compass! Your hand movements will distract your friends so no one will know your secret!

The mini-magnet under your bandage will make the compass go crazy!

Over the Rainbow

What's black and white, but colored all over? Your Color-Changing Chips, that's what! They may start out as black and white, but when you touch them together, they'll become yellow, blue, green, and red! The secret? What else? Hidden magnets!

you'll need...

* ⚹ Color-Changing Chips
* ⚹ Reset magnet

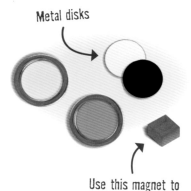

Metal disks

Use this magnet to reset the trick.

get ready

1 Your Color-Changing Chips come with two metal disks: a **white** disk with red underneath, and a **black** disk with green underneath. To begin, put one metal disk on each chip, as shown.

Black covers yellow.

White covers blue.

2 Now both of your chips are black on one side and white on the other. Hold one in each hand, with the metal-disk side facing up. Your thumbs should hold the disks in place.

make magic!

1 Show your friends the chips, explaining that they're black and white. Turn your hands over to show both sides.

2 Turn your hands back over so the metal disks are back on top. Then slide the white side under the black side. The **white** side will change to **blue**!

3 Slide the black side under the blue side. The **black** side will become **yellow**.

 tip For best results, don't let the chips touch until one is directly underneath the other. This will help make sure the metal disk transfers perfectly.

4 For the big finish, turn the chips over to show that the backs have changed color, too!

RESET!

To remove the metal disks, put your reset magnet on the red and green sides and pull the disks off. Easy! Then put the disks back in their starting positions, as shown on the previous page.

Black and Blue

What happens to a black-and-white chip when it bangs into a table? It turns black and *blue*! Well, it *will* if you do a sneaky move with a hidden magnet! Grab a bandage and your mini-magnet, and get ready to learn how to give one of your Color-Changing Chips a magical "bruise"!

you'll need...

* **One Color-Changing Chip (the black-and-blue one)**
* **White disk**
* **Mini-magnet**
* **Bandage**

Stick the mini-magnet to the bandage like this.

get ready

1. Moisten the back of the white disk with a little water or saliva to help it stick. Then put the disk on the blue side of the black-and-blue chip.

2. Put the mini-magnet on the sticky part of the bandage. Then wrap the bandage around the middle section of your right middle finger.

make magic!

1. Hold the chip in your left hand, between your thumb and fingers, with the white side facing the audience.

16

2 Reach across the chip with your right hand and turn it around to show the black side.

3 Then turn the chip one more time so the white side is facing up again.

4 Now for the sneaky magnet move! Reach across the chip as if you're going to turn it around again, but this time touch the magnet to the white disk.

5 When the disk sticks to the magnet, secretly lift it off **as you flip the chip again**. Keep the disk hidden under your fingers!

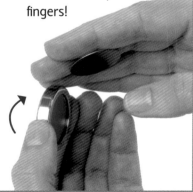

6 Turn the chip all the way around to show the black side again.

Hide the disk under your fingers until step 8. Then slip it into your pocket or brush it into your lap!

7 Slap the chip on the table, with the black side facing up.

8 Tell your friend to turn the chip over as you explain that the chip has turned black and blue because it smacked into the table!

Lonely No More!

The two little red balls that come with your Magic Cup might *look* identical, but they're not. One has a metal core, and the other doesn't. This means that *one* of the balls will stick to the cup's magnetic bottom, and the other won't! You can use this secret to make one ball seem to turn into two!

you'll need...

★ **Magic Cup and Balls**

The bottom of the cup is magnetic, so the trick ball will stick to it.

To figure out which ball is the trick ball (the one with the metal core), drop each one in the cup and see which one sticks.

get ready

1 Put the trick ball in the Magic Cup.

2 Lay the cup on the table, angled so your audience can't see inside. Put the other ball on the table next to the cup.

18

1 Pick up the cup without letting the audience see inside. Then pick up the ball with your other hand.

2 Drop the ball in the cup. Make sure your friends can't see the other ball hiding inside.

3 Put your palm on the mouth of the cup and turn the cup over.

4 Shake the cup so everyone can hear the ball bouncing around inside. Don't worry, the trick ball will stay stuck to the bottom of the cup.

5 Lift the cup off your palm. Everyone will see just one ball.

6 Put the cup back on your palm, using enough force so the trick ball falls away from its hiding place.

Put the cup down HARD!

Keep your fingers curled.

7 Wave your hand over the cup and explain that you're going to use your magic powers to make your little red ball a friend.

8 Lift the cup to reveal both balls!

19

Play a Game of Magic Golf

How do you play Magic Golf? First you hit a ball with an invisible club, and it magically soars from underneath a cup to your pocket. Then you hit the ball back again, and it lands back under the cup! Never played such a crazy game before? Read on to learn the rules!

you'll need...

* Magic Cup and Balls

get ready

1 Put the normal ball (the one *without* the metal core) in your right pants pocket.

2 Then put the trick ball on the table next to the cup, and you're ready to start your first game of Magic Golf!

Trick ball (with metal core)

tip The Magic Cup will work best on a surface that's slightly soft. So, use a tablecloth, or perform the trick on top of a book.

20

make magic!

1 Show the empty cup to your friends, making sure they can see that there's nothing inside (no secret compartments!). Then drop in the trick ball.

2 Grab the cup and turn it over quickly and gently, keeping the cup very low to the table (or your friends will wonder why the ball didn't fall out!). Don't bang the cup hard on the table, or the trick ball will fall off the bottom of the cup.

3 Pretend your hand is an invisible golf club and wave it once over the cup, toward your pocket. Watch your DVD to see how Sofie does this!

4 Then lift the cup a few inches. The ball's gone!

5 Set the cup down hard so the trick ball falls to the table.

6 Now reach inside your pocket and pull out the normal ball. Your friends will think it's the same ball!

7 Put the ball back into your pocket and tell your friends that you're going to hit it back under the cup.

8 Pretend your arm is an invisible club again, and make a swinging motion as if you're hitting the ball from your pocket to the cup.

9 Lift the cup. There's the ball!

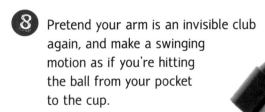

It's Invisi-Ball!

Can a little red ball become invisible and slide through the bottom of your Magic Cup? You can make it *look* that way when you learn a sneaky move that'll make your friends think you took the ball out of the cup. (But really, of course, the ball is stuck to the bottom of the cup!) Try this trick to learn the secrets of invisiball-ity!

you'll need...

* ✱ Magic Cup
* ✱ Trick ball

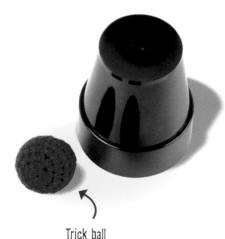

Trick ball

make magic!

1 Hold the cup in your left hand and drop the trick ball inside. Let your friends see it in there for a moment.

2 Turn the cup over on your right palm.

3 Now it's time for a sneaky move called the "Fake Take." Here's how you do it: Pretend to take the ball out of the cup by making a loose fist with your right hand as you move the cup away.

The Fake Take

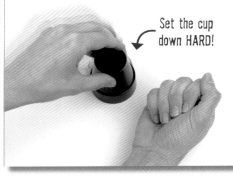

The ball's in here.

But your friends think it's here!

4 Set the cup down hard to free the trick ball. Keep your right hand closed as if you're really holding the ball.

Set the cup down HARD!

5 Tell your audience you're going to make the ball invisible. Then wave your other hand over your fist, like you're working your magic!

6 Open your hand and pretend to pick up the invisible ball.

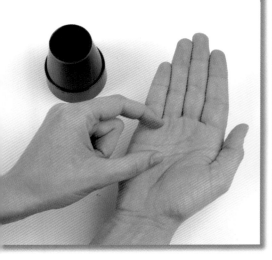

7 Set the invisible ball on top of the cup, and then press on it as if you're pushing it through the cup.

8 Lift the cup. The ball has reappeared!

The Big Surprise

Besides a little red ball (or two!), **what else can you make appear underneath your Magic Cup? How about a marshmallow? An egg? A gum ball? A walnut? A little potato?** *Any* **of these things can appear—just learn the sneaky moves in this trick, and you'll pull off an amazing surprise worthy of a professional magician!**

This is the toughest trick in this book, so it'll take lots of practice. But when you master it, the big surprise will be worth the effort!

you'll need...

* ✶ **Magic Cup**
* ✶ **Trick ball**
* ✶ **The Big Surprise**

Leah uses a marshmallow as the Big Surprise, but check out page 26 for other ideas!

get ready

1 Hide the Big Surprise in your right pants pocket.

2 Set the Magic Cup and the trick ball side by side on a table. You should stand behind the table, and your audience should be **facing you**.

24

make magic!

1 Put the trick ball inside the cup.

2 Do the Fake Take you learned on page 23, pretending to take the ball from the cup.

3 Keep your hand closed and act like you're putting the ball into your pocket.

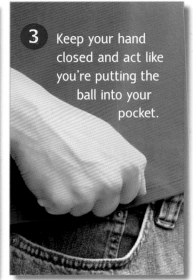

4 Grab on to the Big Surprise, but keep your hand in your pocket.

5 Tell your audience that you're going to make the ball travel from your pocket back to the cup. Make a waving motion from your pocket to the cup, then lift the cup. No ball!

The ball is hiding inside!

6 Pretend you're disappointed that your trick didn't work, and set the cup down hard to free the ball.

7 Now say that you're going to try the trick again, and make another gesture between your pocket and the cup. Remember, this whole time, your right hand is still in your pocket, holding on to the Big Surprise!

Turn the page to learn the next move!

8 Lift the cup to reveal the ball. As you do this, give the ball a little "kick" with the edge of the cup so it rolls away from you, toward your audience.

9 While everyone watches the ball roll, they won't be watching you! Quickly take the Big Surprise out of your pocket. Keep your right hand closed so no one sees anything. Then, quickly put the mouth of the cup in your right hand and sneak the Big Surprise inside it.

10 Grab the rolling red ball with your left hand. As you do this, set the Magic Cup back on the table (with the Big Surprise underneath!). Use your pinky to make sure the Big Surprise doesn't fall out of the cup.

11 Leave the cup on the table. (No one will suspect there's a surprise waiting under it!) Then put the ball in your right hand and stick it in your pocket again.

12 Tell your friends you're going to do the trick again. Make your hand gesture from your pocket to the cup again, and then lift the cup to reveal the Big Surprise!

Try It This Way!

What else can you use for your Big Surprise? Anything that fits inside the cup and your closed hand! Here are just a few ideas:

Small potato

Jawbreaker

Small plum

Gum ball

Egg

The Magical Magnet Ladies

You've seen some of the many ways you can make magic with magnets, but can a magnetic force live inside a magician's *body*?

That's what Lulu Hurst, "The Georgia Wonder," made people believe. Hurst was only fifteen years old when she toured the United States in 1883, but her "Magnetic Lady" act fooled many doctors and scientists.

Lulu Hurst
(1869—1950)

What did Hurst do? In one trick, she would ask a big, strong man to hold a broomstick in both hands. His job was to make sure it didn't move. When Hurst gently placed her hands on it, the stick would tilt in different directions as the man stumbled around the stage trying to keep it steady. Why did this happen? Hurst claimed there was a special "power" inside her that she couldn't explain!

The Little Georgia Magnet

Annie Abbott, another teenage girl who lived in Georgia, watched Hurst do her act. She figured out Hurst's secret and created her own show. Abbott weighed just 98 pounds, so her strength looked even more impressive than Hurst's.

When a group of men were invited to lift "The Little Georgia Magnet" by her elbows, she didn't budge. It was like she was stuck to the floor!

What Was the Secret?

Were the Magnet Ladies *really* magnetic? Nope. Both Hurst and Abbott were able to work with balance, force, and weight in very crafty ways. Hurst knew which direction to push and pull objects to make it look like her volunteers couldn't control them. Annie knew how to shift her weight just a little bit so no one could lift her.

So, as it turned out, the "Magnet Ladies" didn't use (or need!) magnetism at all. But they sure made people *believe* they did!

Hurst used her secret "power" to make it impossible for this man to hold this broomstick steady!

27

Penny Less

In this trick, you'll put six pennies in a cup, **shake 'em up, and pour 'em into a friend's hand.** When your friend counts up the coins, how come there are only five? Because you used a tricky penny shell and a hidden magnet! Try this trick to learn how to make someone magically "penny-less"!

you'll need...

* **Mini-magnet**
* **Bandage**
* **Five regular pennies**
* **Penny shell**
* **Paper or plastic cup**

Mini-magnet
↓

Penny shell
↙

get ready

1 Stick the mini-magnet onto a bandage, as shown on page 10. Then wrap the bandage around the tip of your index finger.

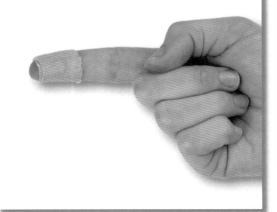

2 Put five pennies on a table and add the penny shell to the group. Then take a seat at the table, and you're all set!

Penny shell
←

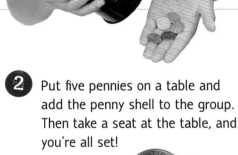

make magic!

1 Hold the cup in one hand with the bandaged mini-magnet touching the side of the cup.

2 Count the pennies and drop them into the cup. When you pick up the penny shell, make sure you don't show the other side to your friends.

3 Shake the pennies around. The penny shell will get stuck to the wall of the cup, thanks to the mini-magnet on the other side!

4 Ask your friend to hold out her hand. Now comes the sneaky part. Dump the coins into her hand and tell her to close her hand right away. Only five pennies will fall into her hand. The penny shell won't fall—as long as you keep your bandaged finger touching the cup!

5 Wave your empty hand over your friend's hand. At the same time, move the cup toward you and hold it over your lap. Lower the cup a little bit so the rim is just below the tabletop.

6 While everyone is looking at your waving hand, pull your index finger away from the cup. The penny shell will fall quietly into your lap.

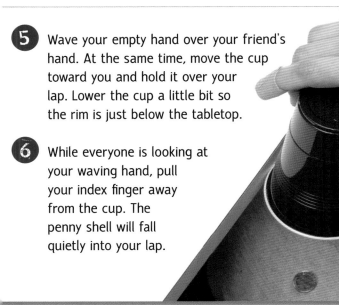

7 Now put the cup on the table. Have your friend open her hand. One of the pennies has disappeared!

Paper Magnet

Magnets pick up all sorts of stuff, like paper clips, pins, and screws. But can a *drawing* of a magnet pick up stuff, too? Sure *can*—with some help from *you*, of course! Just remember to wear your mini-magnet under a bandage on your fingertip. When your friends ask you if it's magnetism or magic, you can say, "It's both!"

you'll need...

* Mini-magnet
* Bandage
* Drawing of a magnet
* Paper clip

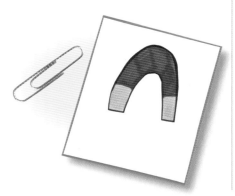

get ready

1 Stick the mini-magnet onto a bandage (as shown on page 10) and wrap the bandage around your index fingertip.

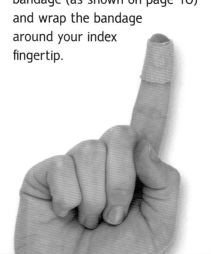

2 Draw a magnet on an index card. Make sure to leave some blank space below the magnet.

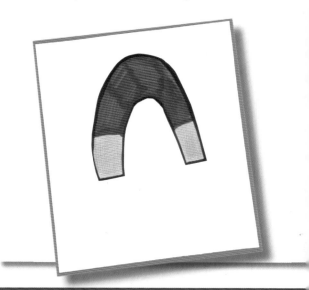

make magic!

1 Hold the card face up with your bandaged finger directly under one end of the magnet drawing.

View underneath

2 Wave your hand over the magnet drawing and say you're going to make it work like a real magnet!

3 Place a paper clip on the magnet drawing, on the part your mini-magnet is touching.

4 Hold the card vertically so everyone can see that the clip is really stuck!

5 Then wave your hand again, saying that you're going to take the magnetic power away. As you do this, move your bandaged finger away from the back of the card.

View from back

6 The clip will fall to the table. No more magnetism!

EXTRA CREDIT ★

What other stuff can stick to your magical magnet? Try a small nail, a hair clip, or a screw. Or try *several* paper clips instead of just one. How many objects can stick to your drawing at the same time?

You Were Magnet-ficent!

So, did you feel the power of magnetism at work when your chips changed color? Did you pull off a big surprise with your Magic Cup? And what about that Penny Transformer Set—were your friends staring in amazement when you turned a penny into a dime?

That's what's so fun about magnetic magic. The magnets do most of the work, and you get *all* the credit!

Want to see what a professional magician can do with magnetic magic? Then check out your DVD, and you'll see Danny perform a routine with a Magic Cup like yours (but bigger). Watch closely, and see if you can figure out his secret moves!

Meet the Magicians

Danny

John

Danny Orleans

Danny is a professional magician who performs all over the country at schools and business meetings. He has a very powerful magnet he uses for special tricks. One time, the magnet got too close to his wallet. Because the magnet was so strong, it erased all the information on his credit cards! That was definitely *not* one of his favorite tricks!

John Railing

John has been a magician for thirty years, performing at parties all over the world. Once he left a magnetic magic trick in his car for a week during a cold Chicago winter. When he tried the trick later, it didn't work. How come? John discovered that freezing temperatures can make magnets lose their strength!